WAR STORIES

COURAGEOUS CHILDREN

Jane Bingham

D1077178

www.raintreepublishers.co.uk
Visit our website to find out
more information about
Raintree books.

To order:
☎ Phone 0845 6044371
🖹 Fax +44 (0) 1865 312263
🖥 Email myorders@raintreepublishers.co.uk

Customers from outside the UK please telephone +44 1865 312262

Raintree is an imprint of Capstone Global Library Limited,
a company incorporated in England and Wales having its
registered office at 7 Pilgrim Street, London, EC4V 6LB –
Registered company number: 6695582

Text © Capstone Global Library Limited 2011
First published in hardback in 2011
Paperback edition first published in 2012
The moral rights of the proprietor have been asserted.

Edited by Louise Galpine and Vaarunika Dharmapala
Designed by Clare Webber and Steve Mead
Original illustrations © Capstone Global Library
 Ltd 2011
Illustrated by KJA-Artists.com
Picture research by Elizabeth Alexander
Originated by Capstone Global Library Ltd
Printed and bound in China by Leo Paper
 Products Ltd

ISBN 978 1 406 22203 6 (hardback)
15 14 13 12 11
10 9 8 7 6 5 4 3 2 1

ISBN 978 1 406 22211 1 (paperback)
16 15 14 13 12
10 9 8 7 6 5 4 3 2 1

British Library Cataloguing in Publication Data
Bingham, Jane.
Courageous children. – (War stories)
303.6'6'083-dc22
A full catalogue record for this book is available from the
British Library.

Acknowledgements
We would like to thank the following for permission to
reproduce photographs: Alamy p. **5** (© Phillip Nicholas
Hodges), **16** (© Pictorial Press Ltd); The Art Archive pp.
8–9 (National Gallery London/Eileen Tweedy), **14** (Culver
Pictures); Canadian Anglo-Boer War Museum p. **12**;
Corbis pp. **4** (© Medford Historical Society Collection), **11**
(Bettmann), **7** (© Stefano Bianchetti), **13** (© Bettmann),
27 (© TWPhoto); Getty Images pp. **17** (Imagno), **19** (Anne
Frank House, Amsterdam), **21** (Joe J. Heydecker/Galerie
Bilderwelt), **24** (Gail Oskin/WireImage); Photolibrary pp.
23 (Nils Jorgensen), **25** (Alain Evrard); Press Association
Images p. **22** (AP); United States Holocaust Memorial
Museum, courtesy of Aviva Kempner p. **18**; Shutterstock
background design and features (© oriontrail).

Cover photograph of two policewomen and a VAD nurse
serving refreshments to young evacuees on 18 June 1940,
reproduced with permission of Getty Images (A. J. O'Brien/
Fox Photos).

We would like to thank John Allen Williams for his
invaluable help in the preparation of this book.

CONTENTS

Words appearing in the text in bold, **like this**, are explained in the glossary.

Look out for these boxes:

WHAT WOULD YOU DO?
Imagine what it would be like to make difficult choices in wartime.

REMEMBERING BRAVERY
Find out about the ways in which we remember courageous acts today.

NUMBER CRUNCHING
Learn the facts and figures about wars and battles.

SECRET HEROES
Find out about the brave individuals who didn't make it into the history books.

INTRODUCTION

It is a sad fact that children have always been involved in wars. Throughout history, children have been innocent **victims** of war and some have even been involved in the fighting. In these terrible situations, many boys and girls have shown great bravery.

Children in battle

In the past, it was not unusual for children to fight in battles. Boys were trained for special jobs in the army, and girls often worked as messengers or spies. Today, there are laws against the use of child soldiers. Sadly, these laws are not always obeyed.

Courageous children

Often, children in war face great danger. They learn to live in frightening situations, and they even risk their lives to save others. This book tells the stories of some truly courageous children.

▶ This is Austin Johnson, a young boy soldier who fought and died in the American **Civil War** (1861–1865).

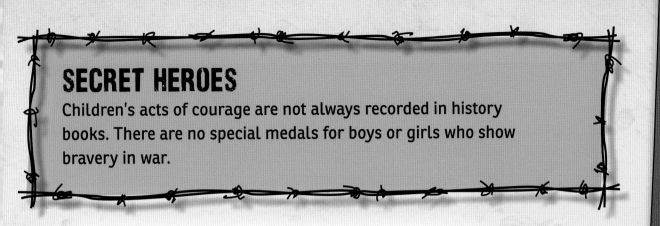

SECRET HEROES

Children's acts of courage are not always recorded in history books. There are no special medals for boys or girls who show bravery in war.

▼ These children are in danger because the adults around them are at war. They are sheltering from gunfire in the West Bank city of Nablus.

CHILDREN IN BATTLES

Ancient armies often included boys. Some carried the armour of adult warriors. Others drove battle **chariots**, and some even had to fight.

How did boys train for battle?

One of the leading armies in ancient Greece belonged to the kingdom of Sparta. Spartan boys began their **military** training when they were just seven years old. They lived in an army camp, and trained hard. They were often forced to go on long marches without any shoes.

▼ As part of their military training, Spartan boys practised wrestling every day.

When they were 12 years old, Spartan boys had to spend a year alone in the wilderness. They had to cope with hunger and cold, and defend themselves from wild animals. At the age of 13, they started to train for war using real weapons. Spartan boys often died during their army training.

REMEMBERING BRAVERY

A famous story about a boy warrior is told in the Bible. David was a young boy who worked as an armour carrier for King Saul. In the Bible story, he fought an enormous warrior, called Goliath, and killed him with a rock shot from his sling.

Squires under fire

In the Middle Ages (from around AD 500 to 1450), boys as young as 14 went to war. They were known as squires and acted as assistants to the **knights**. A squire's training began when he was seven years old.

▼ This painting from the 1400s shows a knight on a white horse riding into battle followed by his squire on a brown horse.

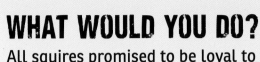

WHAT WOULD YOU DO?

All squires promised to be loyal to their knight. This promise was really tested on the battlefield. Imagine you are a squire and your master is dying from battle wounds. While you are comforting him, an armed man charges towards you. Do you stay with your master? Or do you escape and save your own skin?

On the battlefield

Squires were kept very busy on the battlefield. A squire had to rescue his knight's sword if the knight dropped it. He also had to be ready to hand any extra weapons to his master.

Sometimes, a squire joined in the fighting. He was trained to use a dagger and sword, so that he could help to defend his master.

If a knight was injured, his squire bandaged his wounds. Then the squire stayed with his master until help arrived. If a squire showed outstanding courage, he was rewarded. After the battle, a ceremony was held to make him into a knight.

Before the 1900s, children were often seen on the battlefield. Boys joined the army as drummers or **bugle** players. Girls and boys were often used as spies and messengers.

Willie the drummer boy

One of the most famous drummer boys was 11-year-old Willie Johnston. He fought in the American **Civil War** (1861–1865), a **conflict** between the **Union** and **Confederate** states.

Willie fought for the northern states, and took part in the Battle of Yorktown and the Seven Days Battles. During the Seven Days Battles, his **unit** was forced to retreat under heavy gunfire. Most of the soldiers threw away their equipment so they could run faster, but Willie refused to abandon his drum. He was the only boy who still had his drum at the end of the battle. Willie was rewarded for his bravery by being given a Medal of Honour.

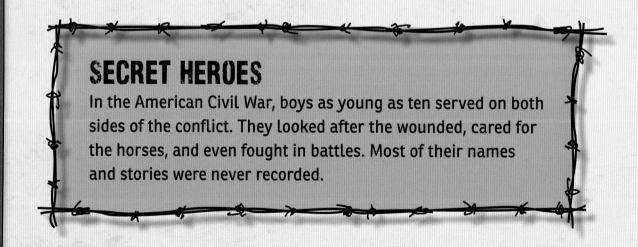

SECRET HEROES

In the American Civil War, boys as young as ten served on both sides of the conflict. They looked after the wounded, cared for the horses, and even fought in battles. Most of their names and stories were never recorded.

▶ This is "Drummer" Jackson. He was a former slave who took part in the American Civil War as a drummer boy. This photograph was used to encourage African Americans to join the war as soldiers.

REMEMBERING BRAVERY

In the 1820s, people in Britain sang a popular song about a drummer boy at the Battle of Waterloo (1815). The song is called "Young Edward" and it begins with Edward marching proudly off to war. At the end of the song Edward dies a "soldier's death" with his head resting on his drum.

"The night was still, the battle hummed,
*   We dug his grave at Waterloo."*

John the bugle boy

Before the days of telephones, army commanders used bugle calls to send signals to their troops. Boys rode around the battlefield, blowing their bugles loudly to tell the soldiers what to do.

John Dunne was a bugle boy who served with the British army in South Africa. In 1899, his army unit was surrounded by enemies. Even though he was fired on from all sides, John kept blowing his bugle. During the battle, John was shot in the arm and dropped his bugle. He was badly wounded, but he still tried to rescue his bugle.

▶ Bugler Dunne was just 14 years old when he went to war. Later, Queen Victoria gave him a silver bugle to replace the one he had lost in battle.

REMEMBERING BRAVERY

When the British people heard about John Dunne's bravery on the battlefield he became a national hero. Shops sold china ornaments of the brave little bugle boy. The ornaments showed John blowing his bugle, with his wounded arm against his side.

Children at sea

Until the 1900s, boys as young as eight years old could join the navy. Even the youngest boys took part in sea battles.

Some boys climbed the **rigging** to look out for danger. They were often shot down or fell to their deaths. Other boys worked as "powder monkeys". Powder monkeys had to load the cannons with gunpowder from nearby barrels. If a spark fell on the gunpowder, the boy was blown to bits.

▶ This young boy was a powder monkey on board the ship USS *New Hampshire* during the American Civil War.

Messengers and spies

During the American Revolutionary War (1775–1783), some courageous children worked as messengers and spies. Their acts of bravery helped American soldiers to overthrow British rule.

John the messenger boy

One young messenger was 14-year-old John Darragh. John's mother, Lydia, gathered news about the plans of the British troops. She wrote this information in **code**, and sewed her messages into buttons on her son's coat. John sneaked through the British army **checkpoints** to reach the American camp. Then the American soldiers removed John's buttons and read the messages.

▶ John's mother, Lydia, entertained British troops in her house and tricked them into telling her their secret plans.

▲ Dicey risked her life in a midnight swim to warn others of danger.

Daring Dicey

Fifteen-year-old Dicey Langston worked as a spy during the American Revolutionary War. One day she learned that supporters of the British were planning to attack a **settlement** on the Enoree River in South Carolina. In the dead of night she swam down the raging river to warn her friends. Thanks to Dicey's courage, many lives were saved.

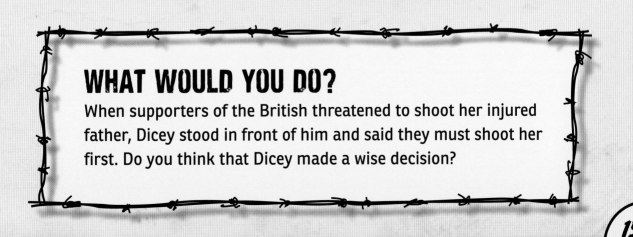

WHAT WOULD YOU DO?

When supporters of the British threatened to shoot her injured father, Dicey stood in front of him and said they must shoot her first. Do you think that Dicey made a wise decision?

CHILDREN IN WORLD WAR II

World War II (1939–1945) began with the rise of Adolf Hitler and his **Nazi** Party in Germany. Hitler aimed to conquer all of Europe. He also planned to wipe out the Jewish people. During the war, children in many parts of the world were killed or injured by bombs, and Jewish boys and girls faced the terrible fate of dying in a **concentration camp**.

▼ The Nazis forced German boys to join the Hitler Youth. This organization prepared them to fight in the army. By 1945, the Germans were running out of soldiers so boys as young as 12 were forced to join the army. Many of them were killed in the fighting.

Krystyna's story

Krystyna Chiger was a Jewish girl from Lvov, in Poland. She was seven years old when her family went into hiding from the Nazis. Her family hid in the **sewers** under the city for more than a year.

Krystyna and her three-year-old brother were terrified. The sewers were very smelly, cold, wet, and dark, and there were rats running around. Even though the children were often scared, they could not cry out in case they were discovered by Nazi guards. They had to stay very still and they could only talk in whispers.

▲ These Jewish children had to struggle to survive after the Nazis arrived in Poland.

Little Joseph

Joseph Schleifstein was only two years old when he and his father were sent from Poland to Buchenwald concentration camp in Germany. The camp guards had instructions to kill all the children, but Joseph's father had a plan for his son. He found a large sack and put little Joseph inside it, warning him to keep absolutely quiet.

Joseph's father was sent to work with a group of Jewish prisoners, and the group helped to keep Joseph hidden. Miraculously, they managed to keep little Joseph safe for the next two years. Joseph was still in hiding at the end of the war when American troops took control of the camp.

When the Americans took over, Joseph was amazed at his freedom. He could run around and make a noise and he no longer felt hungry all the time.

▶ Here little Joseph, wearing his old camp uniform, is being interviewed by a reporter.

REMEMBERING BRAVERY

The story of thousands of children who died in World War II will never be known. But one famous account has survived. Anne Frank wrote a diary describing her life in hiding from the Nazis. The diary covers two years, and ends six months before her death in a concentration camp. Today, Anne Frank's diary is read all over the world.

◄ Anne and her family lived secretly above an office building in Amsterdam, Holland. During the war, Holland was ruled by the Nazis and Jewish people were sent to the concentration camps.

Special scouts

In 1939, Poland was defeated by the Nazis. However, some brave Polish people continued to fight Nazi rule. One important **resistance** group was made up of boys and girls aged between 12 and 17. The group was nicknamed the "Grey Ranks". It was based on the Boy Scout and Girl Guide movements.

The Grey Ranks were divided into senior scouts, aged 15 to 17, and juniors, aged 12 to 14. Senior scouts acted as spies, and deliberately caused trouble for the Nazis. They destroyed German flags, set off fire alarms, and planted stink bombs. Junior scouts ran a secret postal service, delivering messages to members of the Polish resistance.

Finding food

In 1940, the Nazis created the Warsaw **Ghetto** in Poland. This was an area where all the Jewish people in the city had to live. The ghetto was surrounded by high walls and people were not allowed to leave. Inside, there were few jobs and very little food. Many people starved to death.

Some desperate families sent their children out to search for food. Children as young as four left the ghetto secretly. They returned with food that often weighed more than they did.

REMEMBERING BRAVERY

Some photographs of the Warsaw Ghetto have survived. They include pictures of children smuggling food. One photo shows children climbing over the high ghetto wall. Another picture shows a child wriggling through a hole in the wall.

This little boy lived in the Warsaw Ghetto in 1941. He tried to earn some money by playing his violin in the street.

In the years following World War II, there have been many wars around the world. Sadly, all these **conflicts** have involved children as **victims**. In some parts of the world, boys and girls have even joined in the fighting as soldiers.

Kim Phúc's agony

The Vietnam War was fought between North and South Vietnam, with the United States army supporting South Vietnam against the **communist** armies of the north. The war lasted from 1955 to 1975, and many innocent people were caught up in the fighting. Men, women, and children faced horrific attacks from **napalm** bombs, which caused terrible burns.

▲ This photograph of Kim Phúc (centre) was taken just after she and other children had been badly burned by napalm bombs. It made people around the world realize how terrible the war was.

One of the child victims was Kim Phúc. She was with some villagers on a country road, when a pilot dropped his bombs on them. The bombing was captured by a photographer called Nick Út. He also took the injured children to hospital.

Kim Phúc was not expected to live, but she battled to survive. She spent the next 14 months in hospital, and had many painful operations. As an adult, she has devoted her life to supporting child victims of war.

▼ Kim Phúc and Nick Út, who became good friends, stand together with the famous photograph.

REMEMBERING BRAVERY

Nick Út's photograph of Kim Phúc has become world famous. His dramatic image captures a moment of agony and fear. It has become a powerful symbol of the suffering caused by war.

How do child soldiers cope?

Ishmael Beah was 11 years old when **civil war** broke out in Sierra Leone in Africa. Two years later, in 1993, his village was burned down and all his family were killed. Ishmael and some friends wandered around the countryside searching for food and water. In the end they found a village run by soldiers.

The soldiers gave Ishmael and his friends food and shelter, but in return they forced the boys to train for war. Ishmael had to obey all his commander's orders. He was often in danger and he was forced to shoot many people. Ishmael worked as a child soldier for almost three years before he was rescued by a team working for UNICEF (United Nations Children's Fund).

◀ Ishmael has written a book about his experiences. He hopes that it will show other child soldiers that there is life after war.

The UNICEF team took Ishmael to a safe place, away from the fighting. Then they began the process of helping him to recover. Slowly, Ishmael learned to cope with his terrible memories of war. He also prepared for a new life without violence.

▼ This child soldier is from Burma.

NUMBER CRUNCHING

- Around 300,000 children are believed to be fighting in wars around the world.
- Child soldiers are fighting in at least 13 countries.
- Around 30 per cent of child soldiers are girls.

In 1945, at the end of World War II, the world's first **atomic bomb** was dropped on Hiroshima in Japan. The bomb killed over 100,000 men, women, and children. It also poisoned the atmosphere, causing thousands of cases of cancer. The suffering in Hiroshima shocked the world. Many people decided to **campaign** for peace.

Sadako's wishes

One young **victim** of the Hiroshima bomb was Sadako Sasaki. She was two years old when the bomb was dropped, and like many children in Hiroshima during the bombing, she later developed leukaemia (cancer of the blood). By the time she was 12 years old, Sadako knew she did not have long to live, but she wanted to work towards world peace.

Sadako planned to create a thousand cranes, using folded sheets of paper. Cranes are beautiful birds that are seen as symbols of peace in Japan. Each of Sadako's paper cranes represented a wish for peace.

Sadako created 644 cranes before she died. Her friends folded the rest, so that Sadako would have her thousand wishes.

REMEMBERING BRAVERY

After Sadako's death in 1955, children all over Japan campaigned for a monument to be built in her memory. The Children's Peace Monument was completed in 1958 and stands in the Peace Park in Hiroshima. Every year, thousands of children visit Sadako's monument. Each one leaves a paper crane, as a symbol of hope for world peace.

▶ The Children's Peace Monument shows Sadako Sasaki holding up a crane, as a symbol of peace.

COURAGEOUS CHILDREN AROUND THE WORLD

USA
Drummer boy Willie Johnston showed great bravery in the American **Civil War**.

USA
John Darragh worked as a spy during the American Revolutionary War.

USA
During the American Revolutionary War, Dicey Langston swam down the Enoree River, South Carolina, to warn her friends of danger.

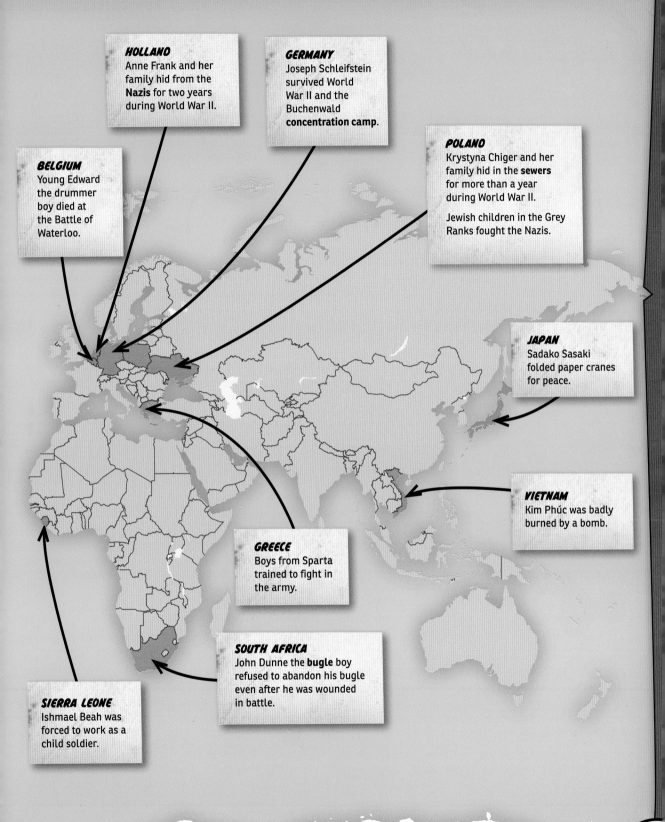

HOLLAND
Anne Frank and her family hid from the **Nazis** for two years during World War II.

GERMANY
Joseph Schleifstein survived World War II and the Buchenwald **concentration camp**.

POLAND
Krystyna Chiger and her family hid in the **sewers** for more than a year during World War II.

Jewish children in the Grey Ranks fought the Nazis.

BELGIUM
Young Edward the drummer boy died at the Battle of Waterloo.

JAPAN
Sadako Sasaki folded paper cranes for peace.

VIETNAM
Kim Phúc was badly burned by a bomb.

GREECE
Boys from Sparta trained to fight in the army.

SOUTH AFRICA
John Dunne the **bugle** boy refused to abandon his bugle even after he was wounded in battle.

SIERRA LEONE
Ishmael Beah was forced to work as a child soldier.

GLOSSARY

atomic bomb very powerful bomb that is made using nuclear power

bugle musical instrument like a small trumpet, used to send signals to troops

campaign take action in order to gain support for a group of people or an idea

chariot small, horse-drawn vehicle used in the past for riding into battle

checkpoint crossing point with guards, where people are checked before being given permission to cross

civil war war between different groups of people within the same country

code letters, numbers, or signs used to send secret messages

communist system of government where one party controls what goods are produced in a country

concentration camp prison camp in which the Nazis held people under terrible conditions, until they died or were killed

Confederate one of the southern states in the United States that wanted to break away and form their own government in the 1800s

conflict fighting or war

ghetto area of a city where people of the same race or colour are forced to live together

knight man of a high social rank who has been trained to fight

military to do with the armed forces

napalm thick, sticky substance made from petrol that is sometimes used in fire bombs

Nazi ruling party of Germany from 1933–1945, or a member of it. The Nazis were led by Adolf Hitler.

resistance organized protest and fighting back

rigging ropes on a ship that support and control the sails

settlement place where a group of people live together

sewer large underground pipes used for carrying waste

Union states that made up the United States after some southern states tried to set up their own government in the 1800s

unit group of soldiers who fight together

victim someone who is hurt, killed, or made to suffer in some way

FIND OUT MORE

Books

Non-fiction

Anne Frank and the Children of the Holocaust, Carol Ann Lee (Puffin, 2008)

Conrad Elroy, Powder Monkey: The Role of the Navy in the American Civil War, Alvin Robert Cunningham (Perfection Learning, 2003)

The Children's War: The Second World War Through the Eyes of the Children of Britain, Juliet Gardiner (Portrait, 2005)

The Diary of a Young Girl, Anne Frank (Puffin, 2007)

Fiction

Mr Lincoln's Drummer, G. Clifton Wisler (Puffin, 1997)

Powder Monkey: Adventures of a Young Sailor, Paul Dowswell (Bloomsbury, 2006)

Websites

www.annefrank.org
Learn all about Anne Frank's short life on this website.

www.bbc.co.uk/schools/primaryhistory/world_war2
Visit this website to find out about children's lives during World War II.

www.pcf.city.hiroshima.jp/frame/kids_e/sadako21.html
This animated website tells the story of Sadako Sasaki, the bombing of Hiroshima, and the creation of the Children's Peace Monument.

A place to visit

The Imperial War Museum
Lambeth Road
London
SE1 6HZ
www.iwm.org.uk

Visit the Imperial War Museum to learn more about the wars discussed in this book.

INDEX